Mourning *the* Loss *of a* Beloved Soul Who Wasn't Muslim

Ten Tools for Healing

by Umm Zakiyyah

Mourning *the* Loss *of a* Beloved Soul Who Wasn't Muslim: Ten Tools for Healing
by Umm Zakiyyah

UZ Courses at **uzhearthub.com** and **uzuniversity.com** RTT Therapy, UZ mentorship, and Feminine Soul Reset at **sqsoul.com**

Translation of meanings of verses from Qur'an adapted from Saheeh International, Darussalam, and Yusuf Ali translations.

Arabic script of Qur'an from legacy.quran.com

Published by Al-Walaa Publications (USA)
Camp Springs, Maryland
Dallas, Texas

TABLE OF CONTENTS

PART ONE: Making Sense of Our Grief　　　5
Bittersweet Memories and Reminders of Loss
PART TWO: Ten Healing Tools　　　12
Spiritual Life Lessons for Grieving Souls
Healing Tool 1　　　13
　It's Okay to Cry and Feel Pain
Healing Tool 2　　　18
　It's Okay to Honor Their Memory
Healing Tool 3　　　25
　Don't Confuse Emotions with Spirituality
Healing Tool 4　　　33
　Respect the Spiritual Etiquettes of Your Faith
Healing Tool 5　　　41
　Refrain from Judging Souls as Good or Bad
Healing Tool 6　　　52
　It's Okay to Hope for the Best
Healing Tool 7　　　57
　The Unseen Is Known to None But Allah
Healing Tool 8　　　62
　Reserve Your Prayers for the Living
Healing Tool 9　　　69
　You Carry the Burden of No Soul But Your Own
Healing Tool 10　　　76
　Let This Be a Beneficial Reminder to Your Soul
Keep reading for excerpt from
He Asked About Islam: Twenty Questions　　　81
　from an American Teen
Read FREE Books by Umm Zakiyyah　　　87
Glossary of Arabic and Islamic Terms　　　88
About the Author　　　90

كُلُّ نَفْسٍ ذَآئِقَةُ ٱلْمَوْتِ وَإِنَّمَا تُوَفَّوْنَ أُجُورَكُمْ يَوْمَ ٱلْقِيَـٰمَةِ فَمَن زُحْزِحَ عَنِ ٱلنَّارِ وَأُدْخِلَ ٱلْجَنَّةَ فَقَدْ فَازَ وَمَا ٱلْحَيَوٰةُ ٱلدُّنْيَآ إِلَّا مَتَـٰعُ ٱلْغُرُورِ ۝

"Every soul shall taste death, and you will only be given your [full] compensation on the Day of Resurrection. And whoever is removed away from the Fire and admitted to Paradise, he indeed is successful. And what is the life of this world except the enjoyment of delusion."
—Qur'an (*Ali 'Imraan*, 3:185)

PART ONE

Making Sense of Our Grief
Bittersweet Memories and Reminders of Loss

"Grief is like a long valley, a winding valley where any bend may reveal a totally new landscape."
—C.S. Lewis, *A Grief Observed*

1

On the afternoon of Sunday, January 26th, 2020, I was sitting in the prayer area of my Maryland home after having prayed *Dhuhr*. I was still doing my daily Qur'an reading after the early afternoon Salaah when my daughter knocked on the door and asked if she could talk to me for a minute. I told her yes.

As she stepped into the room, she asked, "Did you hear what happened?" I told her I didn't know what she meant. "About the basketball player, Kobe Bryant? You knew who he was, didn't you?"

Her use of the past tense confused me momentarily. "Yes…" I said tentatively.

"He died."

For a brief moment, I thought she was mistaken, or that perhaps she had read something from a fake news site. But then she sat next to me and handed me her phone so I could read the news for myself.

As I scrolled through the reports on the screen of my daughter's phone, I slowly processed the weighty reality. Kobe Bryant, as well as everyone else aboard the private helicopter he had been riding in at the time, had died in a tragic accident. I would later learn that his thirteen-year-old daughter was among them.

As the heartbreaking news sunk in, I immediately thought about my own soul and the ever-present shock and pain that death brings, despite it being the only guarantee of life itself. I also thought about loved ones I'd lost over the years, and how I was still making sense of a world without my younger brother, Qaadir, who died in 2008, and my father who had died just six months ago at the time I was processing the news of Kobe Bryant and his daughter.

No matter how familiar death was in the experience of life, it rarely felt familiar, I thought to myself, and it rarely made sense to the human heart.

Today was no different.

Though I was not personally connected to Kobe Bryant and was not much of a basketball fan myself, he had been very much a part of the world I'd known since young adulthood. My heart first became endeared to the basketball player in 1996 after he went to the prom with the singer Brandy. At the time, as I was just twenty years old myself, I thought it was the most heartwarming prom story.

Over the years, Kobe's growing pains and challenges inspired in me a feeling similar to what I'd have for a younger brother, with all its moments of conflicted frustration, hope, and pride.

When you lose someone who touched your life even in a distant way, it's not easy to make sense of your feelings. For reasons that are often inexplicable to us, some deaths of otherwise strangers incite deep emotional pain. Yet other deaths of strangers incite merely a fleeting feeling of distant sadness or momentary self-reflection. Naturally, the more deeply felt the pain, the more challenging and confusing the grief.

When the person who passed away was a close relative, a dear friend, or someone who impacted your life greatly, the pain and grief become even more complicated and deeply felt.

Amongst Muslims, when that deep sadness comes as a result of the passing of a soul who was not Muslim, especially if the person was beloved to us in some way, the feelings that we grapple with can become all the more overwhelming and confusing. Personally, as part of an interfaith family with both close-relatives and extended family who are mostly Christians, I myself know those complicated feelings of overwhelm, sadness, and confusion quite well.

3

In my own life of loss, it has taken me some time to make sense of the complicated emotions I wrestle with as a Muslim grieving a beloved soul who wasn't Muslim. Fortunately, over the years, I've become more familiar with my own grief, and I've found that there are ten tools of healing that help me work compassionately and patiently through the pain.

So, I'm sharing these healing tools here in this book in hopes that they benefit other hurting souls, as they continue to benefit mine:

1. **It's okay to cry and feel pain.**
2. **It's okay to honor their memory.**
3. **Don't confuse emotions with spirituality.**
4. **Respect the spiritual etiquettes of your faith.**
5. **Refrain from judging souls as good or bad.**
6. **It's okay to hope for the best.**
7. **The unseen is known to none but Allah.**
8. **Reserve your prayers for the living.**

9. **You carry the burden of no soul but your own.**
10. **Let this be a beneficial reminder to your soul.**

Dear reader, I pray you find these ten tools of emotional healing and soul-nourishment helpful on your own journey of mourning the loss of a beloved soul who wasn't Muslim.

Whether that person was a close friend or a loved one, or someone who touched your heart and life from a distance, it is my hope and prayer that these ten guidelines can be beneficial emotional and spiritual resources for you.

May our Merciful Creator grant your heart ease and tranquility as you work through the waves of grief amidst your oceans of loss.

PART TWO

Ten Healing Tools
Spiritual Life Lessons for Grieving Souls

"Grief is like the ocean; it comes in waves, ebbing and flowing. Sometimes the water is calm, and sometimes it is overwhelming. All we can do is learn to swim."
—Vicki Harrison

Healing Tool 1
It's Okay to Cry and Feel Pain

"Grief is the last act of love we have to give to those we loved. Where there is deep grief, there was great love."
—unknown

4

Those of us who have non-Muslim family are very familiar with the emotional pain and confusion that comes along with mourning a beloved one who had not accepted Islam. In this, we become accustomed to navigating the delicate space between honoring the affection we have in our hearts for them and submitting to the spiritual etiquette that our faith has outlined for believers when someone has died.

Here, I find it appropriate to share a one-sentence summary from the prophetic guidance that we learn about navigating grief: *The heart aches and the eyes shed tears, but the tongue does not say anything that is displeasing to Allah.*

So, it is completely okay to feel sad and cry, as death is a painful reminder of the fragility of life and how any of us can be literally here today and gone tomorrow. This visceral reality alone is enough to weigh down the heart with sadness and inspire tears to flow from the eyes.

Therefore, sadness and pain should not be viewed as disagreeing with Allah's *qadar* (divine decree). At the same time, it also should not be viewed as representing any right to making a spiritual declaration about the deceased soul.

This is because sadness is completely natural and stems from our complex humanity, whereas spiritual declarations stem from what our Creator has taught us as part of our faith.

5

Sometimes our sadness is rooted in what we will miss about a person. Sometimes our sadness reflects the loss of hopes and dreams we had for that person, whether worldly or spiritual. Sometimes our sadness is rooted in an emotional trigger that is causing us to relive the death of someone we lost previously. Sometimes our sadness is a reflection of deeply feeling our own mortality. And the list goes on.

Just as there are many faces of grief, there are many triggers of grief. And not all of these triggers are directly related to something specific about the person or event that is inciting our sadness and tears.

Sometimes we ourselves do not understand why a particular death affects us deeply while another does not. Whatever is inspiring our emotional pain, it is helpful to remember that we do not necessarily *need* to fully understand our sadness. This is because so much of the human experience exists beyond the realm of conscious understanding. And that's okay. In fact, it is more than okay. This is part of what makes life a beautiful, complicated mystery to the human heart.

In this realm of beauty and mystery, it is quite possible that the Creator Himself has allowed a certain tragedy to touch the hearts of so many as a means of reminding each of us (whether Muslim or non-Muslim) to get our spiritual affairs in order.

This is because it is always helpful for the human soul to be reminded of this ever-present truth of life: The reality of our own death is just a matter of time—which could be sooner rather than later.

Healing Tool 2
It's Okay to Honor Their Memory

"Hold on to the love, not the loss. Grief, I've learned, is really just love. It's all the love you want to give, but cannot. All that unspent love gathers up in the corners of your eyes, the lump in your throat, and in that hollow part of your chest. Grief is just love with no place to go."
—Jamie Anderson

6

During our time in this world, we will benefit from many people who cross our paths, and we'll be inspired by countless more souls more numerous than we can count. Some of these souls we will interact with directly, and other souls we will connect with from afar.

However, how a particular soul touches our life (whether directly or indirectly) is ultimately the decision of our Creator. This is because as humans, we have very little power over the intimate experience of who or what touches our lives and hearts, and we have very little power over exactly how that connection affects us in a specific way.

In His *qadar* (divine decree), our All-Wise Merciful Creator has assigned certain people to be a source of tremendous benefit and inspiration for us, and He has assigned others to be source of severe pain and agony. Each of these trials (in benefit or pain) is part of the tests that Allah has promised humans on earth.

Regarding certain people being placed in our lives as a difficult trial for us, our All-Wise Merciful Rabb says:

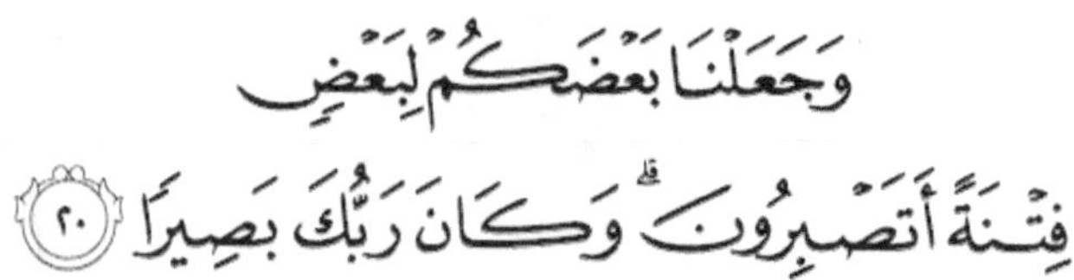

"...And We have made some of you as a trial (*fitnah*) for others. Will you have patience (*sabr*)? And ever is your Rabb (Creator, Owner, and Manager) Seeing."
(*Al-Furqaan*, 25:20)

Here, it is helpful to remember that a *fitnah* (weighty trial) can incite deep pain or harm, or it can incite deep benefit or pleasure. It can also incite a mixture of both. In this *ayah* (divine verse from the Qur'an), our All-Wise Creator is letting us know that no matter what a particular trial incites within us, the purpose of the trial is to test whether or not we will choose *sabr* (patience) in response.

So, as we make the choice of *sabr* in response to our trials of life, it is helpful to remember that although *sabr* means "patience" at its core, *sabr* is so much more than that, as I discuss in the next chapter.

7

I often mention in spiritual discussions this crucial point about *sabr*: Although the term *sabr* is usually translated as merely "patience," in our practical lived experience, *sabr* is three things:

1) withholding ourselves from saying or doing anything that will harm our lives or souls
2) remaining steadfast in saying and doing anything that will benefit our lives or souls
3) getting back up after we fall, and repenting and self-correcting when (not *if*) we make a mistake, lose our way, or sin on this path

And undoubtedly, expressing *shukr* (sincere gratitude) for our worldly blessings is a means of benefiting our souls. So, when we speak of the benefit or inspiration that someone has brought to our lives, whether directly or indirectly, even if that person was not Muslim, this can be a form of showing *shukr* to our Creator. And because this open expression benefits our lives and souls, it is also a type of *sabr*.

Expressing gratitude for the good someone has brought to our life, even if that person wasn't

Muslim, is praiseworthy in our faith because this expression of gratitude is a way of showing gratitude to Allah. This is because *Ar-Rahmaan* (the Most Compassionate and Merciful) is ultimately the One who decreed that we would derive a specific benefit or inspiration from any part of His creation.

When a beloved soul who was not Muslim has been a source of goodness for us, speaking openly about this blessing is also a sign of *emaan* (true faith). Prophet Muhammad (peace and blessings be upon him) taught us: **"Whoever does not thank people has not thanked Allah"** (Sunan Abu Dawud, 4811; *Sahih* by Ahmad Shakir).

Naturally, if a person is alive, we can show gratefulness by thanking them directly. However, when they have passed away, we can show gratitude by speaking of the benefit or inspiration that Allah brought to our lives through them. In this way, we can honor the memory of someone and use this as an opportunity to express *shukr* to our Merciful Creator.

We see an example of this in how the books of prophetic history mention how the Prophet's uncle Abu Talib brought benefit to the believers, and how the Prophet's family, including his parents and his grandfather Abdul-Muttalib, were honest trustworthy people of noble lineage and upstanding character. Honoring this part of their worldly legacy in no way contradicts our recognition of the unseen spiritual reality that pertains to their souls in the Hereafter.

Therefore, it is completely okay to acknowledge the worldly benefit and inspiration that we gain from anyone of Allah's creation. So long as our words and actions are rooted in *sabr* (withholding ourselves from saying or doing anything that will harm our souls), this honorable mention can be a means of thanking our Merciful Creator Himself. This is because deriving worldly benefit and inspiration from each other—irrespective of our varying faiths—is how our Creator has designed the human experience on earth.

Healing Tool 3
Don't Confuse Emotions with Spirituality

"*Emotions can be confusing things, especially when you're sleep-deprived, grieving, hardly able to think.*"
—Shaun Paul Stevens, *Nether Light*

9

When we are in the midst of sadness or grief, especially regarding someone close to our heart, the challenge for the sensitive believing soul is navigating our emotions in a way that is spiritually healthy for us.

In this, we strive to express our emotional pain in a way that nourishes our souls and that refrains from harming our souls. In other words, we strive to express our emotional pain in a way that reflects true *sabr*. In the Qur'an, Allah says:

$$\text{وَلَنَبْلُوَنَّكُم بِشَىْءٍ مِّنَ ٱلْخَوْفِ وَٱلْجُوعِ وَنَقْصٍ مِّنَ ٱلْأَمْوَالِ وَٱلْأَنفُسِ وَٱلثَّمَرَٰتِ ۗ وَبَشِّرِ ٱلصَّٰبِرِينَ ﴿١٥٥﴾}$$

"And certainly, We shall test you with something of fear, hunger, and loss of wealth, lives, and fruits. But give glad tidings to the *saabiroon* (the people of *sabr*)."
(*Al-Baqarah*, 2:155)

In the realm of human emotion, the tragedy of loss is not faith-specific. Worldly loss weighs heavily on anyone, as feeling the pain of loss is merely a manifestation of how Allah created the human heart. In our feelings of sadness, these emotions are not necessarily a reflection of our spirituality. Rather, they are a reflection of our humanity.

In our mortal experience, it is human nature to feel a sense of sadness when we lose something beloved to us. This is the case even when we lose lifeless things such as wealth, a beloved piece of jewelry, a coveted job, or a lucrative opportunity. How much more when that loss involves a human soul?

10

In the *ayah* mentioned in the previous chapter, our Merciful Rabb is reminding us of the nature of life, in all of its agony and loss, and how tragedy will touch every one of us. Sometimes that loss will be of something very close to us, and sometimes that loss will be of something connected to us from a distance. However, in either case, our Creator reminds us that it is only the *saabiroon* (the people of *sabr*) who will derive benefit from these losses.

Specifically, the *saabiroon* are believers whose *sabr* (patient perseverance) is such a defining trait of their heart and lives that the Creator Himself has defined them by their steadfastness in nourishing their souls and protecting their souls from harm.

For the *saabiroon*, the health of their souls consistently takes priority over everything, irrespective of whether this person of *sabr* is enjoying times of ease and happiness, or enduring times of extreme pain and difficulty. In their life of soul-care, an inherent quality of the *saabiroon* is that despite sometimes feeling deeply painful emotions, they consistently channel their pain in ways that nourish their souls and fill their hearts with *emaan* (sincere faith) and inspire their tongues with *dhikr* (sincere remembrance of Allah).

In the Qur'an, Allah describes how the *saabiroon* handle tragedy and loss. He says:

$$ ٱلَّذِينَ إِذَآ أَصَٰبَتْهُم مُّصِيبَةٌ قَالُوٓاْ إِنَّا لِلَّهِ وَإِنَّآ إِلَيْهِ رَٰجِعُونَ ﴿١٥٦﴾ $$

"[They are those] who, when afflicted with calamity, say, 'Truly, to Allah we belong and truly, to Him we shall return.'"
(*Al-Baqarah*, 2:156)

In this *ayah*, Allah is not only describing what is happening on the tongues of the people of *sabr*, but He is also describing what is happening in their hearts.

When the *saabiroon* experience tragedy, their hearts are immediately reminded that everything of this world—whether their wealth and treasured possessions, or the human souls that are beloved to them—are owned by the One who created them and brought them into existence. Therefore, the people of *sabr* realize from the very depths of their hearts that, in their Creator's immeasurable Mercy, Wisdom, and Might, He can do with His creation as He pleases.

Allah says:

$$ أَلَمْ تَرَ إِلَى ٱلَّذِينَ يُزَكُّونَ أَنفُسَهُم بَلِ ٱللَّهُ يُزَكِّى مَن يَشَآءُ وَلَا يُظْلَمُونَ فَتِيلًا ﴿٤٩﴾ $$

"Have you not seen those who claim themselves to be [spiritually] pure (and full of pious goodness)? Rather, Allah purifies whom He wills, and injustice is not done to them, [even] as much as a thread [inside a date seed]."
(*An-Nisaa'*, 4:49)

11

In contrast to the *saabiroon*, those who do not respond to tragedy with *sabr*, their hearts and minds unhealthily fixate on what a certain worldly possession or beloved human soul meant to them and others in this world. As a result, nearly all of their sadness and grief is rooted in a form of unhealthy emotionalism that spills into their spiritual experience in a damaging way.

In this space of suffering that is not rooted in *sabr*, the grieving soul uses his or her emotions to make sense of the world of spirituality, instead of using his or her spirituality to make sense of the world of emotions. It is in this unhealthy space that the unsettled *nafs* (inner self and soul) expresses anger, frustration, or disagreement with Allah's *qadar*. Or this *nafs* makes emotional proclamations regarding the unseen spiritual world that they imagine (or are convinced) awaits the one they loved or admired.

If we fall into this spiritual and emotional confusion—as so many of us are naturally inclined to do in times of grief—here is where we begin speaking about how we know this "good soul" will be in

Paradise or how we know this "good person" will be rewarded immensely by God for all the good they've done. These proclamations are often expressed as a means to soothe our own aching hearts. In our grief, our pain and longing are inciting an unhealthy emotional state that is more deeply connected to our love and hope for creation than a healthy spiritual state that is more deeply connected to our love and faith in our Creator.

For this reason, it is crucial for the believing soul to consistently strive and pray for sincere *sabr*, as the absence of true *sabr* could mean filling our hearts with a form of unhealthy emotionality. And when our emotions take over, our emotions begin to guide our spirituality, instead of our spirituality guiding our emotions.

Healing Tool 4
Respect the Spiritual Etiquettes of Your Faith

"Boundaries define us. They define what is me and what is not me. A boundary shows me where I end and someone else begins… Knowing what I am to own and take responsibility for gives me freedom. Taking responsibility for my life opens up many different options. Boundaries help us keep the good in and the bad out."
— Henry Cloud, *Boundaries*

12

Respecting the spiritual etiquettes of our faith means owning and honoring our spiritual boundaries. Without these boundaries, our emotionality can fuel our spirituality until our personal feelings, limited knowledge, and human judgment replace the all-encompassing wisdom, limitless knowledge, and divine justice of Allah.

When our emotionality begins to fuel our spirituality, we begin to view the world from the lens of human judgment instead of divine judgment. Consequently, our entire understanding of even the unseen spiritual world is viewed through this inverted lens.

This is how so many of us become genuinely confused as to how a "good person" could ever be denied Paradise after they die. This is also how so many of us feel emboldened to openly proclaim that a person we've labeled as "good" will in fact enter Paradise or will "rest in peace" in their graves. Oddly, we proclaim this about the *ghayb* (unseen) even without having any certain knowledge of this person accepting *emaan* (authentic spirituality) while they were alive.

Yet in the Qur'an, our All-Wise Creator and Master of the Day of Judgment says:

إِنَّ ٱلدِّينَ عِندَ ٱللَّهِ ٱلْإِسْلَٰمُ

"Truly, the [only] *deen* with Allah is Islam..."
(*Ali 'Imraan*, 3:19)

As is well known in Islam, the Arabic term *deen* refers to each person's spiritual way of life, religion, or set of beliefs and life-guiding behavior codes that they adopted in this world. Regarding the option to choose a spiritual way of life other than Islam, Allah says:

وَمَن يَبْتَغِ غَيْرَ ٱلْإِسْلَٰمِ دِينًا فَلَن يُقْبَلَ مِنْهُ وَهُوَ فِى ٱلْآخِرَةِ مِنَ ٱلْخَٰسِرِينَ ﴿٨٥﴾

"And whoever seeks a *deen* other than Islam, it will never be accepted of him, and in the Hereafter he will be one of the *khaasiroon* (people who suffer the ultimate loss)."
(*Ali 'Imraan*, 3:85)

Specifically, the *khaasiroon* are those who experience ultimate spiritual loss in the Hereafter and will never enter Paradise, despite all of the apparent good they did while they were on earth.

13

The religious perspective that ultimate spiritual loss is linked to one's disbelief in a specific faith and that ultimate spiritual success is linked to one's belief in a specific faith is not unique to Islam. It is in fact an inherent characteristic of all Abrahamic faiths (i.e. Judaism, Christianity, and Islam).

Despite the fact that modern day Judaism and Christianity have strayed from the pure monotheistic teachings of the Prophets Moses and Jesus (peace be upon them), the modern practice of these faith traditions still retain some remnants of their roots in *Tawheed* (worship of Allah alone) and Islam (submission to Allah alone and belief in all of His prophets and messengers).

One such monotheistic root shared by all Abrahamic faiths is this foundational religious belief: Spiritual atonement in the Hereafter is a divine gift granted exclusively to true believers. In this, only those believers in God who had a sincere, enduring relationship with their Creator that was rooted in *emaan* (authentic spirituality and true faith) will be granted the everlasting gift of Paradise.

Additionally, this sincere *emaan* that earns a believing soul the merciful gift of living eternally in Paradise is not a type of faith that humans can accurately measure or define. Rather it is defined, measured, and known exclusively and most intimately by only God Himself.

14

In the divine definition of *emaan*, all of a person's goodness emanates from the faith in their hearts. As such, all of a person's worldly deeds stem from this spiritual root and are thus judged based on a person's core spiritual reality.

This is why in Islam, like all Abrahamic faiths, so much emphasis is put on the opportunity for forgiveness, atonement, and mercy instead of on a human being's inherent goodness itself. In the spiritual realm, there is no ultimate human goodness except when it stems from a sincere, humble connection to one's Creator.

In light of this, we can understand the deep spiritual wisdom behind each faith tradition having very specific acts of worship and spiritual etiquettes that are unique to it—especially at the moment after which a soul has transitioned from its worldly home and is embarking on the first step toward its everlasting home in the Hereafter.

After our private worship and spiritual beliefs themselves, how this moment of death is handled by the living is arguably the most obvious manifestation of our own spirituality on earth. Therefore, when a person dies, those whose hearts truly believe in their own faith traditions will sincerely and humbly respect the spiritual etiquettes and boundaries of their faith.

As such, we begin to understand that there is a very practical, spiritual reason that funerals are hosted by the faith community of the deceased, not by anyone else. This is the case no matter who the deceased's family was or how much others outside their faith loved and admired them in this world.

Thus, Jews do not host funerals for Christians and Muslims, and Christians do not host funerals for Jews and Muslims. This is because it is well known that funerals are fundamentally acts of worship.

In these acts of worship, formal prayer services are held for the deceased and are conducted based on very specific beliefs about the unseen journey of the soul. So naturally, these formal prayers for the soul mirror what that deceased person himself or herself actually believed in this world.

Therefore, refraining from offering official prayers or from hosting the funeral services or memorials of someone outside our faith merely respects this religious reality. It also reflects our acknowledgement of not only what the deceased themselves believed while they were alive, but also our respect for the spiritual etiquettes and boundaries of our own faith tradition.

Nevertheless, as Muslims, we fully acknowledge that we have no certainty of knowledge regarding the spiritual state in which someone has died, no matter what religion (or lack thereof) they ascribed to in this world. Hence the healing tool that I discuss in the next section: *Refrain from judging souls as good or bad.*

Healing Tool 5
Refrain from Judging Souls as Good or Bad

"By Allah, other than Whom there is nothing and no one worthy of worship, verily one of you behaves like the people of Paradise until there is but an arm's length between him and it, and that which has been written overtakes him, and so he behaves like the people of the Hellfire and thus enters it. And verily one of you behaves like the people of the Hellfire, until there is but an arm's length between him and it, and that which has been written overtakes him and so he behaves like the people of Paradise and thus he enters it."
— Prophet Muhammad, peace be upon him
(Bukhari and Muslim)

15

As Muslims, when we refrain from offering prayers or memorials for souls outside our faith, this does not necessarily point to any definite unseen reality about the state of their souls. Rather it points to our own heart's humble and sincere respect for our own faith and the guidelines of our Creator.

Therefore, when we do not offer official prayers for non-Muslim souls, we are not claiming to know that a particular person was ultimately "bad" or "good" in front of his or her Creator. This is because, in the end, only Allah knows the exact state that was written for each soul at the time of death.

In fact, as the famous prophetic hadith mentioned at the beginning of this section quite profoundly alludes to, there will be people who lived their entire lives as Muslims, yet right before their souls are taken, they abandon their faith and thus face eternal punishment in the Hereafter. Similarly, there will be people who lived their entire lives as disbelievers, yet right before their souls are taken, they repent and submit to Allah and thereby fulfill the spiritual requirements of true faith as defined by Allah. As a result, they enjoy the divinely gifted eternal abode of Paradise after they die.

Even still, in all likelihood, the Muslim funeral prayer would have been performed for the former soul, and no Muslim funeral prayer would have been performed for the latter soul. Yet in front of Allah, the former was a disbeliever while the latter was a believer. Nevertheless, whenever someone dies, we treat them according to what was apparent to us in this world, as this is the only sensible way to treat another human soul. Beyond that, we are not responsible for unseen spiritual realities that are known only to Allah.

At the same time, given the fact that we fully and humbly recognize our limited knowledge as it relates to other human souls, we as Muslims refrain from openly judging souls as good or bad, even those who were apparently not Muslim. In other words, no matter what is "obvious" to our own limited human perception regarding someone else, we refrain from what is often referred to as "playing God."

16

So often in life, we advise each other, "Don't judge!" intending to remind each other that ultimate judgment of someone is reserved for God alone. However, in times of death, we often forget that this same advice applies, even when speaking about those people we perceive as "good souls."

In other words, just as we are forbidden from casting judgment on someone as being ultimately "bad," we are also forbidden from casting judgment on someone as being ultimately "good." The only exception to this is when specific personalities are mentioned by name as being "bad" or "good" in the divine texts.

For example, in the Qur'an, Allah refers to the severe punishment that the tyrannical Pharaoh of Egypt, along with his followers, will receive on the Day of Judgment. This is due to his rejection of Prophet Moses (peace be upon him) and his tormenting and killing the believers who chose to believe in Allah and follow Prophet Moses:

وَوَقَىٰهُ ٱللَّهُ سَيِّئَاتِ مَا مَكَرُوا۟ وَحَاقَ بِـَٔالِ فِرْعَوْنَ سُوٓءُ ٱلْعَذَابِ ۝

ٱلنَّارُ يُعْرَضُونَ عَلَيْهَا غُدُوًّا وَعَشِيًّا وَيَوْمَ تَقُومُ ٱلسَّاعَةُ أَدْخِلُوٓا۟ ءَالَ فِرْعَوْنَ أَشَدَّ ٱلْعَذَابِ ۝

"...And the people of Pharaoh were enveloped by the worst of punishment. The Fire, they are exposed to it morning and evening. And the Day the Hour appears [it will be said], 'Make the people of Pharaoh enter the severest torment.'"
(*Ghaafir*, 40:45-46)

Amongst those specific souls who have been firmly established as good in front of Allah are the wife of Pharaoh and Maryam (Mary) the mother of Jesus (peace be upon them). Allah says of them:

وَضَرَبَ ٱللَّهُ مَثَلًا لِّلَّذِينَ ءَامَنُوا۟ ٱمْرَأَتَ فِرْعَوْنَ إِذْ قَالَتْ رَبِّ ٱبْنِ لِى عِندَكَ بَيْتًا فِى ٱلْجَنَّةِ وَنَجِّنِى مِن فِرْعَوْنَ وَعَمَلِهِۦ وَنَجِّنِى مِنَ ٱلْقَوْمِ ٱلظَّٰلِمِينَ ۝

وَمَرْيَمَ ٱبْنَتَ عِمْرَٰنَ ٱلَّتِىٓ أَحْصَنَتْ فَرْجَهَا فَنَفَخْنَا فِيهِ مِن رُّوحِنَا وَصَدَّقَتْ بِكَلِمَٰتِ رَبِّهَا وَكُتُبِهِۦ وَكَانَتْ مِنَ ٱلْقَٰنِتِينَ ۝

"And Allah presents an example of those who believed: the wife of Pharaoh, when she said, 'My Lord, build for me near You a house in

Paradise and save me from Pharaoh and his deeds and save me from the wrongdoing people.' And [the example of] Mary, the daughter of 'Imran, who guarded her chastity, so We blew into [her garment] through Our angel [Gabriel], and she believed in the words of her Lord and His scriptures and was of the devoutly obedient."
(At-Tahreem, 66:11-12)

There are many other examples throughout the Qur'an and prophetic Sunnah where specific people were mentioned due to their established goodness, such as all of Allah's Prophets and Messengers. There are also many other examples throughout the Qur'an and prophetic Sunnah where specific people were mentioned due to their established evil, such as Abu Lahab and his wife. Therefore, it is only these specific people and groups of people whom we are allowed to assign the ultimate label of "good" or "bad."

17

No matter how sincere our intentions or how deep our grief, whenever we delve into judging specific souls as "good" or "bad" in this world, we are treading a very dangerous path. In this dangerous path, we are assigning to ourselves—due to the thoughts and perceptions of our own minds and due to the emotions and feelings within our own hearts— perfect divine knowledge and wisdom.

When we fall into this, this is often due to our assignment of exaggerated importance to certain ostensible traits of someone or something they've done. These are characteristics or actions that we observed in a person while he or she was alive. In this, we often assign exaggerated importance to a specific event that we witnessed or to a specific experience we had with this person during their lifetime. As a result, as a mere creation of Allah, we fail to comprehend these three basic, fundamental realities of life:

1) *What is most important to you is not necessarily what is most important to our Creator.*

2) *Your experience with someone does not necessarily reflect their actual spiritual reality or their soul's true experience in relationship to Allah.*

3) *Even for those deeds that the person did that were quite obviously good or bad, you do not know the intentions in that person's heart, and you do not know whether or not they repented (or regressed into sin and evil) before they died.*

It is only when we forget these basic spiritual truths that we become distressed regarding how a "good person" could ever be denied Paradise or how a "bad person" could ever be granted Allah's mercy and forgiveness.

For the self-honest soul, the question then becomes "How are *you* defining human good or evil?" When we are honest with ourselves in response, we see quite clearly that the answer to this question is rooted in our own limited worldly experience and in our own limited human perception.

18

In this world, there are undoubtedly many ostensibly charitable, selfless activists and "good people" who are beloved and admired by nearly everyone in their families, circles, and communities. At the same time, it is well-known that many of these "good people" who are known by these traits are *also* those who are unkind, neglectful, or abusive to many innocent souls. Additionally, they might be simply indifferent toward the people they are responsible for, or they might carry an air of entitlement when they are interacting with loved ones.

In other words, when it comes to so many people who are known to the world (and even to many in their families) as "good souls," in their most intimate spaces, they are often emotionally unavailable, unkind, neglectful, or even intentionally harmful or abusive.

On those rare occasions that we become aware of any of this hidden harm, we do not continue to label these wrongdoers and abusers as "good people." This, despite the inescapable fact that many people will continue to genuinely see them as such.

Moreover, even when others know about the harm they've caused and try to use the good these people have done as a way to cancel out the significance of their wrongdoing and abuse, we ourselves would likely struggle deep inside with actually seeing these wrongdoers and abusers as "good people."

While there might indeed be people who genuinely believe that someone's public kindness and "goodness" cancels out any consistent wrongdoing to loved ones or other innocent souls in private, this is not how our Creator defines human goodness. Similarly, while there may indeed be people who genuinely believe that someone's beautiful relationship with creation and their generosity toward others should overshadow any consistent wrongdoing to their souls in private, this is not how our Creator defines piety or spiritual sincerity.

In this, it is well known that it is how we show up in our most intimate worldly spaces—where there are no cameras, accolades, or lauding audiences—that most accurately reflects who we "really" are as a person deep down. Similarly, it is how we show up in our most intimate spiritual spaces—where there is no audience except your own soul and the Creator Himself—that most accurately defines who we "really" are as a person in front of our Rabb.

For this reason, the wise believer refrains from making any definitive claims about another person's inner state, whether this person is alive or has passed away. This is because life experience and intuitive wisdom has taught the sincere soul that we have no way of truly knowing who is (or is not) "good" or "bad" in truth.

Healing Tool 6
It's Okay to Hope for the Best

"If there is any possible consolation in the tragedy of losing someone we love very much, it's the necessary hope that perhaps it was for the best."
— Paulo Coelho

19

As we strive to respect the spiritual etiquettes of our faith and stay clear of "playing God" by declaring the ultimate goodness (or badness) of a human soul, it's okay to hope for the best for someone. This is where our hearts hope that a person who was ostensibly non-Muslim privately accepted Islam before their death.

However, in respecting the spiritual etiquettes of our faith, it is not correct for a believing soul to formally act on this hope by offering formal prayerful supplications, funeral programs, memorial services, prayer vigils, or anything else in the realm of worship. This is because acts of worship are by their nature faith-specific, and our Creator has not legislated this sort of response to the death of a non-Muslim soul, no matter how beloved they were to us.

In our *deen*, our spiritual way of life in Islam, it is well known that all acts of worship have the general ruling of being forbidden unless there is specific evidence for them in the Qur'an or prophetic example. And other than showing respect for a deceased soul and speaking with gratitude about their observable worldly deeds that we've benefited from, it is a part of *sabr* to refrain from any formal acts of worship that honor the *spiritual state* of someone outside our faith.

20

Nevertheless, even as we maintain *sabr* while our hearts hope for the best, it is important to understand that our choice to refrain from formally praying for a beloved non-Muslim soul does not grant us permission to speak ill of them in any way.

Our Mother Aa'ishah (may Allah be pleased with her) said that Prophet Muhammad (peace and blessings be upon him) said, **"Do not abuse the dead, for they have reached what they put forward"** (Ṣahih al-Bukhari, 1329).

In this merciful prophetic advice, we are reminded that every deceased soul is seeing the results of their deeds, for better or worse, so there is no need for us to use our tongues to speak on this matter of the unseen. As such, our spiritual obligation on earth is merely to refer to the spiritual etiquettes of our faith in responding to what has been made apparent to us.

Those who apparently lived as believers in this world will be granted the formal prayers and funeral services that beseech our Merciful Creator to shower forgiveness and mercy upon their souls. In contrast, those who apparently lived as disbelievers in this world are granted the respect of silence regarding their spiritual state—even as we are free to hope in our hearts that they had a good end.

Healing Tool 7
The Unseen Is Known to None But Allah

"Say, 'None in the heavens and earth knows the unseen except Allah, and they do not perceive when they will be resurrected.'"
— Qur'an (*An-Naml*, 27:65)

21

It is true that our faith has very specific spiritual etiquettes in response to a person's death, and in this, our formal prayers are reserved for only known believers. At the same time, as alluded to earlier, this spiritual etiquette does not negate the fact that there will indeed be professed Muslims we pray for in this world, but who will never enter Paradise due to dying in a state of *kufr* (disbelief). This because for some people we've come to know as Muslims, their actual spiritual state at death is in direct contrast to their apparent spiritual state during their lifetime.

Similarly, as alluded to earlier, there will indeed be those who for all appearances were non-Muslims in this world, and thus, we refrain from formally praying for them after their deaths. However, unbeknown to us, they actually died in a state of *emaan* (Islamic spirituality), while no one knew this about them except Allah.

Therefore, it becomes obvious that our choice to pray for a certain soul cannot possibly benefit them if their heart had no *emaan* during their life. Likewise, our choice to refrain from praying for a soul cannot possibly harm them if they died upon *emaan* without our knowledge.

Yet still, we submit to the spiritual etiquettes of our faith, as this is a form of submission to our Creator.

22

That the unseen spiritual reality of someone's soul sometimes contradicts what our spiritual etiquette would seem to suggest about them teaches us this: *When it comes to acts of worship, the primary purpose of them is submission to Allah, not human declaration of the unseen.* This is a point worth repeating over and over to the confused human heart.

In fact, it is a foundational trait of *taqwaa* (God-consciousness and protecting the soul from harm) to humbly acknowledge the *ghayb*, which encompasses all unseen realities that are beyond human knowledge, perception, understanding, and comprehension. This belief in the *ghayb* relates to both worldly and spiritual matters that exist in Allah's infinite awareness yet are beyond our realm of limited human awareness.

Interestingly, this belief in the *ghayb* is the first trait of the people of *taqwaa* that Allah mentions in the entire Qur'an. Additionally, it is also this trait that is amongst those that clearly distinguish between those who will benefit from the spiritual guidance of Allah's revelation and those who will not.

Allah says in the Qur'an:

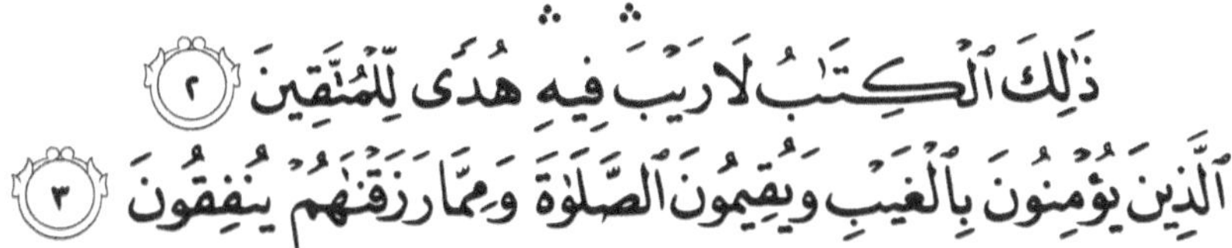

"This is the Book whereof there is no doubt, a guidance to those who are *muttaqoon* (people of *taqwaa*). [They are those] who believe in the *ghayb* (unseen), establish Salaah, and spend out of what We have provided for them."
(*Al-Baqarah*, 2:2-3)

Although *taqwaa* is often translated as God-consciousness or piety, it encompasses the way in which sincere believing souls live spiritual lives wherein they continuously protect their own souls from harm. And part of protecting our souls from harm is believing in the *ghayb* while openly acknowledging that the intricate details of the unseen, such as the state of someone's soul, are known to none but Allah.

Healing Tool 8
Reserve Your Prayers for the Living

"Give someone a hug today. Those you cannot reach with your arms, reach with your hands—in sincere du'aa (prayerful supplication). Pray for them. Pray for their guidance. Pray for their healing. Pray for their peace. Pray for their happiness and success in this world and in the Hereafter. This is how you hug a soul, even when they are out of reach."
— from the journal of Umm Zakiyyah

23

When my daughter told me of the death of Kobe Bryant and I read about his and his daughter's tragic deaths online, I was heartbroken for his widowed wife and the other children he left behind. In moments like these, it's so easy to romanticize a person. It's so easy to glorify the life they lived, or even allow our hearts to turn them into "saints" or "angels."

However, the truth is, like the rest of us, they were complex, beautifully flawed human beings with a deluge of faults, imperfections, and sins that we know nothing about. It just so happens that they passed away, and we're amongst the ones left behind. None of this automatically means anything negative about them as people, of course. But it's also true that their soul being taken before ours doesn't automatically elevate their spiritual status.

The truth is that for no human soul does death turn us into flawless, faultless creation, and it most certainly doesn't turn us into "saints" or "angels." This is the case whether any of us passes away due to natural causes, is killed, dies suddenly, or is taken from us by suicide.

So, here's a gentle reminder I give my hurting soul in moments of grief: *Let's not overpraise the dead, even if you are passionate about what they stood for and even if you feel sympathy for what they suffered in life.*

But here's what we *can* do, especially for those who did not accept Islam before they passed away: If they have loved ones who are left behind, we can pour our love and compassion into them. We do this by, for example, showing up for them in ways that help them through this difficult time.

We can also healthily channel our grief for the loss of their loved one through praying for *them*. In this, we can pray for the spiritual guidance of those left behind, and we can also pray that this tremendous loss will be a cause for those left behind to draw closer to their Merciful Rabb in this world and in the Hereafter.

24

The inalterable reality of life is this: We are all going to die. As the saying goes, "None of us is getting out of here alive."

After our inevitable death, we must all stand before our Creator and answer for our deeds—and not all of us will have heavy scales of *good* deeds. Thus, not all of us enter Paradise. So, the most we can do for someone who has died is pray for them and their forgiveness—that is, if they died upon *emaan*.

And the most we can do for *ourselves* is to live our lives correctly before our souls are taken and we are lowered beneath the ground.

But before that inevitable moment of transition into the next stage of our soul's journey, it's important not to tell ourselves that death in itself is a rite of passage into sainthood or elevated spiritual goodness. Additionally, it's important not to tell ourselves that death in itself is a testimony to the praiseworthiness of someone's life.

In the end, death is only a "rite of passage" to never again having a single moment of life or breath left. So, there will be no more opportunities to change, to better yourself, or to repent before your soul leaves the body.

25

We can love someone intensely, in life or death, but this love cannot transform the reality of their inner spiritual world. Moreover, it cannot change the very real private reality of their relationship (or lack thereof) with their Creator.

Here's something I wrote in my journal years ago as a reminder to my own restless soul: *Neither your love for someone nor their apparent kindness or goodness cancels out their shirk or disbelief.*

Allah says,

إِنَّمَا ٱلْمُؤْمِنُونَ ٱلَّذِينَ ءَامَنُوا۟ بِٱللَّهِ وَرَسُولِهِۦ ثُمَّ لَمْ يَرْتَابُوا۟

"Only those are believers who believe in Allah and His messenger then doubt not..."
(*Al-Hujuraat*, 49:15)

As alluded to in earlier chapters and bears repeating over and over again in hopes that the repetitive reminder benefits the sincere believing soul: In Islam our choice to pray for someone or refrain from praying for someone is more about the spiritual state of our own souls than it is about theirs.

This is because a heart that is filled with true *emaan* knows that all spiritual goodness is ultimately rooted in submitting to the decree of Allah. This means respecting the spiritual etiquettes that He's decreed as part of our faith in this world. This also means respecting the unknown spiritual reality that He's decreed for all human souls in the Hereafter.

In other words, how we handle the death of someone is a test for our own souls, not a declaration about theirs.

In this, our Creator is placing in our lives a trial to see if we will have *sabr*—in refraining from saying or doing anything, except in direct response to what has been made apparent to us—while leaving the unseen reality of their souls to Allah.

As such, if we sincerely wish to offer prayers for someone after a non-Muslim soul has passed away, these prayers should be reserved for the living. Here, we can pray that this painful tragedy is a means of spiritual and emotional healing for the loved ones who were left behind (or for anyone touched by the loss). We can also pray that this deep emotional pain serves as an incentive toward spiritual guidance and religious self-correction in all of our lives.

Healing Tool 9
You Carry the Burden of No Soul But Your Own

> *"First, you are only responsible for yourself. You cannot control the world, or other people, only yourself. Therefore, your only focus should be on maintaining control of three things: your thoughts, your attitudes and your actions."*
> — Joshua Craft, *The Way to Live*

26

All of these spiritual lessons teach us that it is not upon us to stress over someone else's spiritual relationship with their Creator. No matter how much we loved or admired them in this world, navigating their spiritual reality is a burden that was placed on their soul and their soul alone—just as the burden of your soul was placed on you and you alone. And only Allah knows how each of us has fulfilled this weighty responsibility, or not.

Here's something that we can add to what was discussed earlier: Just as we do not pass judgment on any soul by claiming them to be ultimately good or bad, we do not pass judgment on any soul by claiming that they were "Muslim in their heart" or a "sincere believer." This is especially the case when they themselves did not proclaim *emaan* while they were alive.

This spiritual etiquette is directly connected to the necessity of separating our emotional feelings from someone else's spirituality. This is the case even as it relates to apparent believers in God from a different faith tradition, especially if we experience them as sincere. For example, these believers in God could be ostensibly good Jews and Christians we've met in real life or any other religious people whom the Qur'an might describe as "People of the Book" or "People of the Scripture."

The challenge is, when we see how apparently sincere or God-conscious a person from the "People of the Book" was throughout their life, it is tempting to genuinely feel that we *know* they were amongst the sincere believers. But the truth of the matter is, we do not *know* this. Rather, we deeply *feel* this. While there's nothing wrong with this deep feeling, it's helpful to remember this: Even as it relates to our deep feelings about ourselves in this world, rarely can we accurately discern the *actual* spiritual sincerity of our own hearts and souls.

How much more is this the case as it relates to the heart and soul of someone else?

27

What causes many sincere Muslims confusion regarding the true faith of beloved souls amongst the People of the Book is that the Qur'an describes *some* of them as true believers. This Qur'anic description is about the sincere Jews and Christians whom Allah Himself counts as believers who will enter Paradise after they die. This is due to their genuine belief in Allah and the Last Day and having adhered to the pure, authentic teachings of the Prophets Moses and Jesus (peace be upon them) while they were alive.

Upon reading these *ayaat* (divine verses) about the truthful followers of these earlier Prophets and Messengers, some Muslims interpret this divine spiritual reality as human permission to apply this description to any People of the Book. Therefore, so long as *we* personally experienced them as a "good person" in this world, we begin to feel that it's okay to describe these Jews and Christians as believers.

In this mindset, many of us treat any "good" Jew or Christian who has passed away just as we would any of our deceased brothers or sisters in Islam. Thus, upon this person's death, we grant this non-

Muslim all the spiritual rights that Allah has reserved exclusively for the people of *emaan*, such as offering formal prayers for them, participating in (or hosting) memorial services in their honor, and openly praying for their forgiveness and entry into Paradise.

In these moments, no matter how heavy our hearts feel at the loss of a loved one or a beloved soul from the People of the Book, it is essential that even amidst our heartfelt grief, we connect to our spirituality more than our deeply felt emotions. In this, we rely on the definition of *emaan* as shared with us by Allah in the Qur'an, instead of relying on the emotional hopes of our grieving hearts.

Allah says,

إِنَّكَ لَا تَهْدِى مَنْ أَحْبَبْتَ وَلَٰكِنَّ ٱللَّهَ يَهْدِى مَن يَشَآءُ وَهُوَ أَعْلَمُ بِٱلْمُهْتَدِينَ ٥٦

"Verily, you do not guide whom you love, but Allah guides whom He wills. And He knows best those who are guided."
(*Al-Qasas*, 28:56)

28

From a spiritual perspective, if there is any topic that is quite clear and unambiguous in the Qur'an, it is that which distinguishes *emaan* (true faith) from *kufr* (disbelief). In these Qur'anic definitions of *emaan*, none allow us to rely on only our hopes and feelings about someone when we're ascertaining their Islam (sincere submission to God).

Nonetheless, even if we were to interpret the *ayaat* in the Qur'an about the believers from the People of the Book as referring to the religious Jews and Christians of today, their belief would be subject to the same conditions as any other believer. In these conditions of *emaan*, even a professed Muslim who has declared the *shahaadah* (formal testimony of Islamic faith) falls outside the fold of Islam if he or she disbelieves in anything from the Qur'an, even a single *ayah*.

How much more so a person who disbelieves in *all* of the Qur'an? How much more so a person who has in fact heard of Prophet Muhammad (peace and blessings be upon him) yet has chosen a *deen* (a spiritual way of life) other than Islam?

Nevertheless, it is understandable that our heavy hearts wish to assign Islam to a loved one due to our deep love for them. Yet Allah says,

إِنَّمَا ٱلْمُؤْمِنُونَ ٱلَّذِينَ ءَامَنُوا بِٱللَّهِ وَرَسُولِهِ ثُمَّ لَمْ يَرْتَابُوا

"The believers are only the ones who have believed in Allah and His Messenger and then doubt not..."
(Al-Hujuraat, 49:15)

Healing Tool 10
Let This Be a Beneficial Reminder to Your Soul

وَذَكِّرْ فَإِنَّ الذِّكْرَىٰ تَنفَعُ الْمُؤْمِنِينَ ۝

*"And remind, for indeed, the reminder benefits the
believers."*
— Qur'an (*Adh-Dhaariyaat*, 51:55)

29

When we are faced with painful tragedy or loss, it is helpful to see this experience as an opportunity to remind ourselves of the weighty affair of our own human soul. In the Qur'an, Allah says,

$$\text{كُلُّ نَفْسٍ ذَآئِقَةُ ٱلْمَوْتِ وَإِنَّمَا تُوَفَّوْنَ أُجُورَكُمْ يَوْمَ ٱلْقِيَـٰمَةِ فَمَن زُحْزِحَ عَنِ ٱلنَّارِ وَأُدْخِلَ ٱلْجَنَّةَ فَقَدْ فَازَ وَمَا ٱلْحَيَوٰةُ ٱلدُّنْيَآ إِلَّا مَتَـٰعُ ٱلْغُرُورِ ﴿١٨٥﴾}$$

"Every soul shall taste death. And only on the Day of Resurrection shall you be paid your wages in full. And whoever is removed away from the Fire and admitted to Paradise, he is indeed successful. The life of the world is only the enjoyment of deception."
(Ali 'Imraan, 3:185)

So, as we mourn the loss of any beloved soul, we should bear in mind that regardless of *their* spiritual reality and ultimate fate in front of Allah, we ourselves are still alive in this world. Therefore, we should stay vigilant to the numerous ways in which our own hearts and lives can become entangled in this "enjoyment of deception."

In enjoying the pleasurable *ghuroor* (deception) of this world, it is so easy for our hearts to become addicted to the glitter, success, and temporary comforts of our earthly existence. In this natural tendency toward self-deception, we can begin to genuinely imagine that all human goodness stems from these experiences—with regards to our own personal and spiritual legacy, as well as that of others.

However, in truth, what is most urgent in times of loss is to bear in mind that there is no guarantee that we ourselves will "rest in peace" after we die. Therefore, we should humbly and sincerely pray for our own souls, begging Allah to make us amongst those who are forgiven and thus granted the spiritual honor of peacefully returning to our Creator at death.

This, so that when someone prays for us, speaks well of us, or says, "May they rest in peace," it will reflect not only the spiritual etiquette of their faith, but also our spiritual reality beyond this world.

30

In closing, I offer this heartfelt *du'aa* for you, dear reader. This is something I wrote in my personal journal years ago and shared in *Dear Struggling Soul*:

Dear struggling soul, this is my prayer for you...

May every trial you face in this confusing world be a means for you to draw closer to your Merciful Rabb in this world and in the Hereafter.

If your heart is hurting or breaking, may He heal it and grant you tranquility and peace. If you are battling loneliness and are longing for companionship, may He grant you a soul companion who will be a comfort and a mercy to you in this world and your companion in Paradise.

If you have suffered loss and have no idea how you'll go on, may He grant you better than you lost and reunite you with the believers amongst His beloved in this world and in the Hereafter.

If you are battling spiritual confusion, emptiness, or frustration, may He gift you with the light of emaan,

and may He make the coolness of your eye the
Salaah and the spring of your heart the Qur'an…

Until you meet Him.

And for those heartfelt prayers that you've
whispered to Him on the edge of desperation, tears
in your eyes, begging of His bounty and mercy, may
He grant you what your heart desires—and may He
grant you better than the best you could hope for or
imagine.

And may your last days be the best of your life, your
last deeds your best deeds, and your best day the
Day you meet Ar-Rahmaan.

And dear struggling soul, may the Most Merciful
write you down amongst those whom He loves,
announcing your name above the heavens and
commanding the angels to love you as He loves you,
until love of you is placed in the hearts of His
believers on earth.

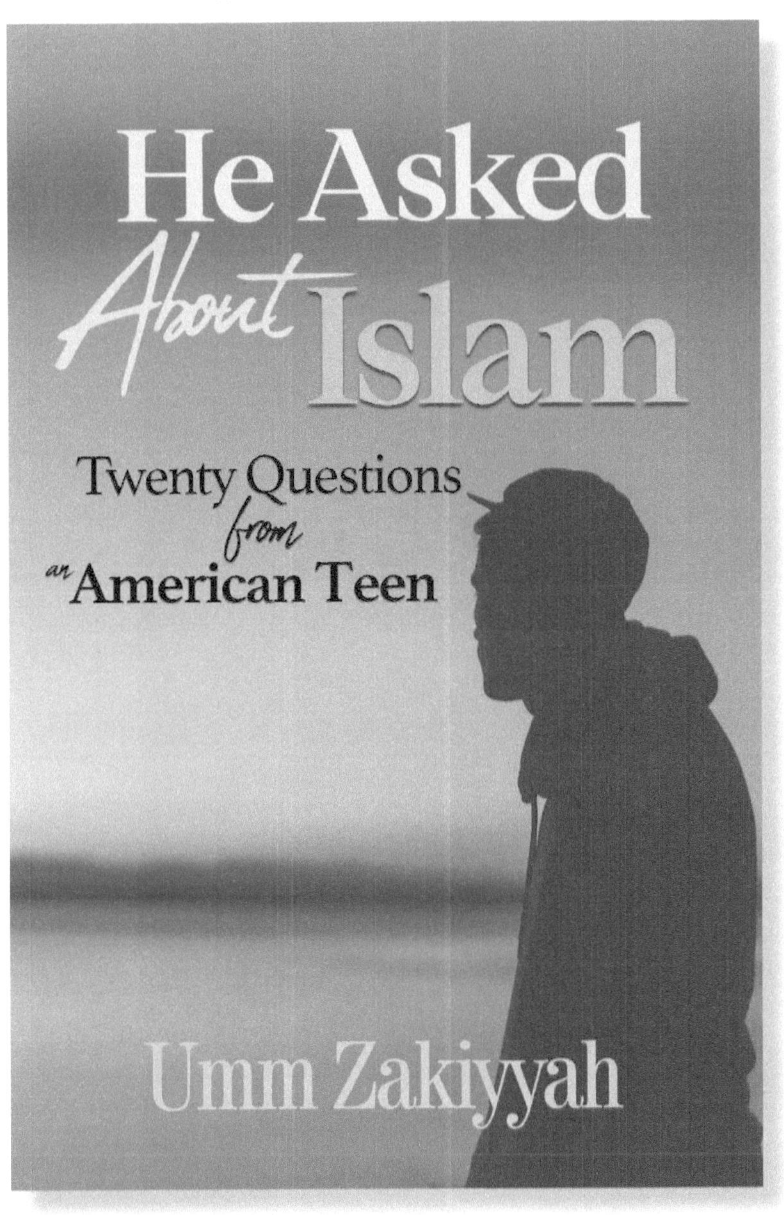
He Asked
About Islam
Twenty Questions
from
an American Teen
Umm Zakiyyah

An American high school student was given the homework assignment to interview someone from a different faith, and he chose Muslims. Here are his questions and my answers.

PART 1
Allah and Life After Death

"Say: He (God) is Allah, the One and Only. Allah, the Eternal Refuge. He neither begets nor is born And there is none co-equal or comparable unto Him."
—Qur'an (112:1-4)

"How can you disbelieve in Allah? Seeing that you were without life and He gave you life. Then He will cause you to die, then again bring you back to life [for Resurrection] and unto Him you will return."
—Qur'an (2:28)

Question 1. Who is your God and why do you worship Him?

My God is the Creator of the heavens and the earth. He is the Creator, Owner, and Manager of all that exists, from what we see and from what we don't see, from what we know and from what we don't know. God (whom we call "Allah" in Arabic) is the God of all people—you, me, and all humans who have ever walked the earth. I worship Allah because He alone has the ability to hear and answer prayers and reward worship in this world and in the Hereafter.

Question 2. How can you get to know your God better?

We come to know Allah better in three ways:

1) Reflecting on His signs all around us and within us: He created the heavens in the sky, the ground beneath our feet, and even the hearts in our breasts. These signs remind us that Allah created all of this and us for a very important purpose.
2) By praying to Him directly and asking for His guidance in all affairs: We do this by calling on Him alone, without the aid of "saints," prophets, or anything of His creation or our imagination.
3) Studying from the two revelations He has given to humans as a guide until the end of time, the Qur'an and the Sunnah: The Qur'an is the final holy Book revealed to Allah's Messenger, Prophet Muhammad, peace be upon him; and the Sunnah is God's Wisdom that inspired the life, words, and actions of Prophet Muhammad.

Question 3. What do you have to do to live a good life in the eyes of your God?

Allah requires us to do only this to live a good life: Believe in Him as He has asked us to, follow what His Messenger taught us, and continually repent from the mistakes and sins that we will all make while we live on this earth.

In the Qur'an Allah says,

> **"Say [O Muhammad to all people], 'If you [really] love Allah, then follow me. Allah will love you and forgive you your sins. And Allah is Oft-Forgiving, Most Merciful."**
> *Ali'Imraan,* 3:31

Question 4. Where do you go after you die and how do you get there?

After we die, all humans enter the grave, where they will remain until the Last Day. The first part of this journey begins when the Angel of Death seizes our soul until no more life remains in our limbs. We are then placed beneath the soil of the earth, our graves. Once there, we are asked three questions by the angels Munkar and Nakir pertaining to the life we lived on earth: *Who is your Lord? What is your religion?* and *Who is your Prophet [sent to you]?*

Humans remain in these graves until Allah resurrects all descendants of Adam. On this tremendous day, the bones will be reassembled, and they will be clothed with flesh and skin like we had in this world. During this resurrection, we will come from our graves in a drunken state, caused by the trepidation that afflicts us in the heart-wrenching knowledge that we must face our Lord for Judgment regarding how we passed our lives in this world.

Allah says,

> **"Does man think that We shall not assemble his bones? Yes, We are Able to put together in perfect order the tips of his fingers."**
> *Al-Qiyaamah*, 75:3-4

We arrive at this point of resurrection as a result of our Creator simply saying "Be!" and it will be done.

The Day of Judgment stretches out for what would account for 50,000 years in this world. On this somber day, the sun will be drawn close to the earth such that the heat becomes excruciating. No one will be exempt from the distress suffered at this moment except those who lived a life of belief and righteousness in the world.

Read more at **uzauthor.com**

Read FREE Books by Umm Zakiyyah

Glossary of Arabic and Islamic Terms

Allah: Arabic term for God; the only One who has the right to be worshipped

Ar-Rahmaan: Name of Allah meaning The Most Merciful, Most Compassionate

'aqeedah: foundational beliefs of the Islamic spiritual way of life

ayaat: plural form of *ayah*

ayah: verse from Qur'an or divine sign

deen: spiritual way of life; religion

Dhuhr: midday prayer in early afternoon, the second of the five foundational prayers in Islam

du'aa: prayerful supplication; informal prayer

emaan: sincere faith; authentic spirituality; belief in Islam; *Tawheed*

fitnah: difficult trial

ghayb: unseen world and reality known only to Allah

ghuroor: spiritual self-deception

khaasiroon: people who suffer the greatest loss in the Hereafter

kufr: disbelief in Islam; spiritual blasphemy; any belief, speech or action that cancels one's *emaan*

nafs: human inner self made up of the complex interconnectedness of a person's soul, mind, heart, and body

qadar: divine decree; predestination

Rabb: another name for Allah that refers to His Lordship over creation; Creator, Owner and Manager of all that exists

saabiroon: believers who are distinguished by their patient perseverance in life; people of *sabr*

sabr: sincere patience; patiently persevering upon that which benefits one's life and soul, and patiently persevering in abstaining from that which harms one's life and the soul

Salaah: the five foundational daily obligatory prayers in Islam: *Fajr, Dhuhr, 'Asr, Maghrib,* and *'Ishaa'*; second pillar of Islam; any formal prayer, whether optional or obligatory

shahaadah: formal declaration of faith that marks one's entry into Islam: "I bear witness that nothing has the right to be worshipped except Allah alone, and I bear witness that Muhammad is His slave and messenger"; sincere testimony of *Tawheed* recited repeatedly throughout a Muslim's life

shukr: sincere gratefulness, thankfulness or gratitude

tafseer: authentic interpretation and spiritual explanation of the *ayaat* of Qur'an

taqwaa: sincere God-consciousness and daily soul care that protects the heart from corruption and the soul from spiritual harm in the Hereafter

Tawheed: Oneness of Allah; singling out the Creator alone in worship; authentic monotheism; sincere belief in the Oneness of Allah

About the Author

Known for her soul-touching books and spiritual reflections on emotional healing, Umm Zakiyyah is a world-renowned author, speaker, and soul-care mentor. She specializes in supporting women of faith transform into the best version of themselves—personally, emotionally, and spiritually.

Also known by her birth name Ruby Moore and her "Muslim name" Baiyinah Siddeeq, Umm Zakiyyah is the internationally acclaimed, award-winning author of more than forty books, including novels, short stories, and self-help. Her books are used in high schools and universities in the United States and worldwide, and her work has been translated into multiple languages.

Her novel *His Other Wife* is now a short film (available on Prime Video).

Umm Zakiyyah is certified in Rapid Transformational Therapy ® (RTT) and hypnotherapy, qualifications she earned under the guidance of Marisa Peer, author of *I Am Enough*.

Umm Zakiyyah is a certified member of IACT (International Association of Counselors and Therapists) and an executive member of IICT (International Institute of Complementary Therapists).

Umm Zakiyyah studied Arabic, Qur'an, Islamic sciences, *'aqeedah,* and *tafseer* in the USA, Egypt, and Saudi Arabia for more than fifteen years.

Umm Zakiyyah has a BA degree in Elementary Education, an MA in English Language Learning, and Cambridge's CELTA (Certificate in English Language Teaching to Adults).

She is currently based in Dallas, Texas (USA).

Connect with her online:
UZ books: uzauthor.com
Therapy, coaching, and mentorship: sqsoul.com
UZ courses: uzhearthub.com and uzuniversity.com
Instagram: @uzauthor